decorative
lighting

Ideas & Projects

Better Homes and Gardens Books
Des Moines, Iowa

Better Homes and Gardens® Books
An imprint of Meredith® Books

Decorative Lighting Ideas & Projects
Editor: Brian Kramer
Art Director: The Design Office of Jerry J. Rank
Contributing Editor: Shelley Stewart
Contributing Writer: Louis Joyner
Copy Chief: Terri Fredrickson
Copy and Production Editor: Victoria Forlini
Editorial Operations Manager: Karen Schirm
Managers, Book Production: Pam Kvitne, Marjorie J. Schenkelberg
Contributing Copy Editor: Kim Catanzarite
Contributing Proofreaders: Dan Degen, Heidi Johnson, Erin McKay
Indexer: Sharon Duffy
Electronic Production Coordinator: Paula Forest
Editorial and Design Assistants: Kaye Chabot, Karen McFadden, Mary Lee Gavin

Meredith® Books
Publisher and Editor in Chief: James D. Blume
Design Director: Matt Strelecki
Managing Editor: Gregory H. Kayko
Executive Editor, Home Decorating and Design: Denise L. Caringer
Director, Operations: George A. Susral
Director, Production: Douglas M. Johnston
Executive Director, Sales: Ken Zagor

Vice President and General Manager: Douglas J. Guendel

Better Homes and Gardens® Magazine
Editor in Chief: Karol DeWulf Nickell

Meredith Publishing Group
President, Publishing Group: Stephen M. Lacy
Vice President-Publishing Director: Bob Mate

Meredith Corporation
Chairman and Chief Executive Officer: William T. Kerr

Chairman of the Executive Committee: E. T. Meredith III

contents

getting started

Bring your home to life with interior lighting that gives form and texture to a room, warms a dark corner, highlights a favorite piece of art, or creates just the right mood. You can build in ceiling lights and sconces or choose lamps that complement your home's architecture and fit your decorative style. **Remember that lighting isn't used only at night.** Even during the day you need well-planned interior lighting to **balance and augment sunlight.** For interiors, there are **three main types of lighting: general, task, and accent.** Each has a different purpose. **General lighting, also called ambient lighting, is the overall lighting** that, for example, enables you to see and walk safely through an otherwise dark room. **General lighting should not intrude** but rather remain a quiet, subtle presence. **Task lighting, as the name implies, provides a more intense light** that helps you see while concentrating on the

things you need to do. Reading, sewing, cooking, and studying all require task lighting. **Task lighting can be as simple** as a table lamp sitting beside your favorite chair or as elaborate as a system of spotlights above a kitchen work surface. **Accent lighting provides the extra touches that make a room sparkle.** You can add a tiny lamp to a bookshelf, mount a picture light over a family portrait, or place softly glowing candles around a bathtub. **Accent lighting can also be built in.** Fixtures recessed into the ceiling are used to accent a painting, emphasize surface texture, or make a hall more interesting with pools of light. Wall-mounted sconces can frame a mantel or flank a doorway. **Control the mood of a room with**

dimmers that adjust light levels to the desired intensities with the touch of a finger. Notice how the tone of the light grows warmer as you turn down the brightness. **The lightbulbs you choose affect the color and quality of the light as well.** Halogen bulbs offer a crisper, whiter light than do conventional incandescent bulbs, making halogens a popular choice for accenting collections of china or glassware. Study the Lamps, Overhead Fixtures, and Special Effects chapters for **ideas and inspiration, as well as special projects** and information on **lighting fundamentals.** The Entries, Living Rooms, Dining Areas, Kitchens, and Bed & Bath chapters focus on **special requirements for these particular rooms.** The Special Places chapter offers suggestions for lighting your library, home office, and reading nook. **Lighting is a marvelous and powerful decorating tool**—learn to use it well, and your home will look and function the way you've always hoped it would!

lamps

More flexible than any other lighting, table and floor lamps require no installation. Simply plug them in and turn them on—but pay attention to their height, light, and style.

lamps

On the previous two pages, small lamps function mainly to create a mood, especially in the evening, with low-level bulbs and unique shades. Consider how the lamps shown here, *clockwise from upper left*, are also suitable for their purposes:

● Although one is a table lamp and one a floor lamp, these two fixtures create visual balance in a traditional room because they are close in height and have matching translucent silk shades.

● While not necessary during the day because of abundant natural light, at night this lamp captures incandescent light with an opaque shade, angling it toward the two chairs for reading.

● Ginger-jar lamps do double duty as they target their light toward a pair of back-to-back sofas, each of which can accommodate readers. Even behind a single sofa, a slim table is a handy location for lamps, books, or other items.

● Dark corners benefit dramatically from well-placed light fixtures. While spotlighting the large Staffordshire dog on its base, this lamp illuminates the whole area for reading and conversation.

● Tucked beneath the steep slope of an attic ceiling, this cozy nook has room for a desk and a comfortable lounge chair. Because the contemporary metal lamp bends so readily, its light can be adjusted for reading without the ceiling interfering.

● Positioned above and over the shoulder for good reading light, this floor lamp has a three-way switch for versatility. Use the highest setting for reading, a lower one for general lighting, and the lowest for conversational lighting.

Every style has its place, but a lamp needs to be the right choice for its function as well. *Clockwise from upper left:*

A contemporary floor lamp combines the flexibility of a swing-arm light with the upward-directed light of a torchère, providing enough bright light for reading as well as overall illumination.

One can never have too many choices—this bed boasts a pair of table lamps and supplemental lighting from independently controlled, adjustable sconces aimed downward for reading.

In this bedroom, a slim table lamp on one side and an equally slim floor lamp on the other create a casual, asymmetrical balance. When not used for reading, the floor lamp can be lowered.

Three fixtures on one mantel create an undeniable focal point with vibrant lighting. A pair of tall lamps flanks the painting, which is lit from above by a picture light attached to its frame.

Controlled by a dimmer, a small uplight commonly used to illuminate plants backlights two sculptures on top of the tall cabinet.

A pair of matching, eye-level table lamps brightens an antique dressing table whose trifold mirrors reflect the light and visually expand the room.

A beaded shade complements a frosted glass tabletop. Before buying such a shade, however, try it out with the bulb you plan to use. Some shades are more decorative than functional; they let far too much light through and work best with low-wattage bulbs.

lampideas&projects

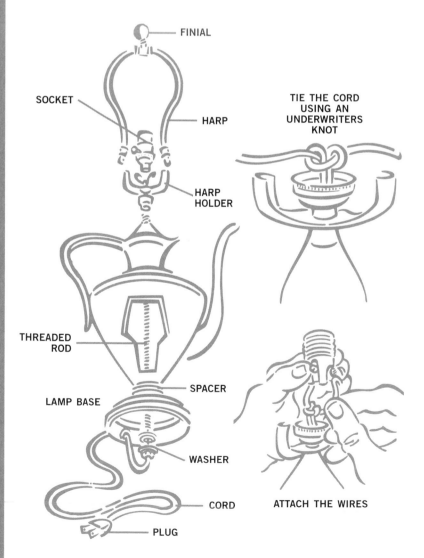

FINIAL

SOCKET

HARP

HARP
HOLDER

THREADED
ROD

LAMP BASE

SPACER

WASHER

CORD

PLUG

TIE THE CORD
USING AN
UNDERWRITERS
KNOT

ATTACH THE WIRES

BASIC LAMP WIRING: HOW TO MAKE A LAMP FROM ALMOST ANYTHING

■ **Drill a hole** through the object from top to bottom; a drill press works best for an accurate lineup. Tough or fragile surfaces sometimes require specialized drill bits, for instance rugged bits for masonry or diamond-coated bits for porcelain.

■ **Choose a cap and base** that complement the shape of the lamp and will cover the drilled holes. Many caps and bases are commercially available.

■ **Purchase a lamp-wiring kit,** a standard threaded rod, washers, and the harp holder at a home improvement or hardware store. Specialized parts, such as decorative bases, spacers, and finials, are available at lamp shops.

■ **Stack the components,** including the socket and harp, and measure the height from top to bottom; add only enough rod height for the rod to screw into the metal components and subtract enough for the bottom of the rod to recess ¼" from the bottom of the base (drill a 1"-wide and ½"-deep recessed area in the underside of the base, if needed, to make it sit flat). Use a hacksaw to cut a standard threaded rod to this measurement.

■ **Decide where you want the cord to exit** the lamp base. If the lamp has feet, leave the cord loose; otherwise drill an exit hole in the back of the lamp base.

■ **Insert the rod** through the base, the drilled object, and the cap. Secure the cap and base with a washer. Thread the electrical cord through the rod. Screw the rod through the harp holder and into the bottom portion of the metal socket; then tighten them securely. Carefully pull apart a few inches of the cord to separate the two wires; tie the wires into an underwriters knot. Strip off about ¾" of the plastic covering at the ends and attach the bare wires beneath the socket screws with a screwdriver. Add a plug to the end of the cord.

■ **Attach the harp,** insert a bulb into the socket, and then test it. Add a shade and secure it with a decorative finial.

BEFORE YOU SHOP FOR A LAMP

Although its style is usually the first thing you notice, if a lamp turns out to be unsuitable for your needs, you won't like it for long. Avoid problems by planning ahead. Or, if you already have lamps, adapt them so they provide better light. Use the drawings and measurements *right* to help you plan.

■ **Consider the height.** Ideally, a reading lamp is situated beside the chair so light pours over the shoulder. The bottom of the shade reaches seated eye level for maximum light and minimum glare. Consider whether you're likely to be sitting or standing when applying makeup or doing other close work and plan the lamp height accordingly. For these situations it's better to choose lamps with translucent shades.

■ **Measure before buying a table lamp.** Before heading to the stores, measure the piece of furniture upon which the lamp will sit. Then measure each lamp you're considering from its base to the bottom of the shade. You want the combined height of these two measurements to be around 40 inches (seated eye level).

■ **Many lamps have multiple functions.** Consider how you'll use a lamp before choosing one. Will it provide light for reading? If so, search for one on which the bottom of the shade comes to approximately seated eye level. Will it throw light onto the ceiling, or will it be used only to lighten a dark corner? Then you'll want something taller or perhaps one with a torchère shade that aims light upward.

■ **Plan ahead for built-ins.** Position wall-mounted lamps as described above and in the drawings *right*. Because built-in lamps aren't movable unless they have swinging arms, always allow enough space between them. Few things are more discomforting than being crowded by lights or facing directly into a glare.

DESIGN TIP Some people need more light to see but are also more sensitive to glare. Aim for more overall room lighting and avoid shadowy areas that force the eye continually to adjust between bright and dark.

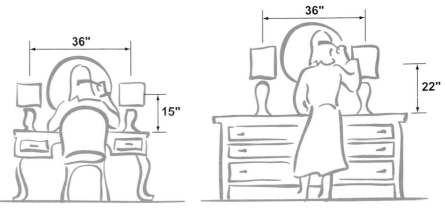

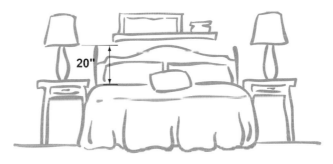

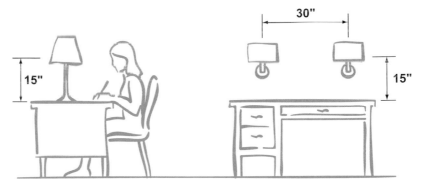

COMPARING LIGHTBULBS

■ **Brightness.** Although most people think of bulbs in terms of wattage, light output is actually measured in lumens, a measure of brightness noted on the bulb packaging. When comparing the amount of light different types of bulbs produce, compare lumens, not watts.

■ **Cost.** Budget-conscious people will want to compare the costs of using various bulbs. Your electric bill reflects the total energy consumed, so it's often wise to use bulbs that give you the most lumens per watt, even if those bulbs cost more to buy. As a rule, incandescent lights are the least energy-efficient; fluorescent and halogen bulbs with screw-in bases fit many of the same lamps and give the same light at less cost. Because they don't get as hot as incandescent bulbs, fluorescent bulbs also last much longer.

■ **Color and shape.** Many people prefer the slightly gold-toned light that incandescent bulbs provide. Another plus is that they come in many different shapes. On the other hand, fluorescent bulbs emit light that looks "cooler," and only a limited range of screw-base shapes fit in lamps (some bulbs are too tall for the existing lampshade to cover them). Low-voltage halogen lights, also available with screw-in bases, produce a whiter, brighter light, but the choice of bulb shapes is limited. Many newer lamps are designed to use halogen bulbs.

BULBS: COMPARING POWER, LIGHT, AND LIFE

INCANDESCENT	FLUORESCENT
60 WATTS	**15 WATTS**
840 lumens	925 lumens
1,000 hours	10,000 hours
75 WATTS	**20 WATTS**
1,170 lumens	1,200 lumens
750 hours	10,000 hours
100 WATTS	**30 WATTS**
1,690 lumens	1,850 lumens
750 hours	10,000 hours

PLANNING YOUR RECEPTACLES

As portable and versatile as it may be, no electric lamp can emit light unless it's plugged into a receptacle (often called an outlet; technically, an outlet is anywhere that electricity exits wiring including appliances, fixtures, and receptacles). Most homeowners tend to take the humble receptacle for granted until they belatedly discover that there is not one where they need it. Planning receptacles as part of a building or remodeling project, or hiring a professional electrician to install additional outlets, will alleviate this problem.

■ **Building and remodeling.** The U.S. building code requires that every room have enough receptacles so no point on a wall is more than 6 feet from an outlet; your local code may be different. During construction, you can add extra locations. Place a receptacle *at least* every 6 feet on every wall, including exterior walls. If a wall between two doors is at least 2 feet wide, it should have a receptacle too. The standard distance from the floor is 12 to 16 inches.

■ **Don't strain your back.** Avoid having to move a bed or heavy piece of furniture in order to plug in or remove a pair of lamps. Install two wall receptacles or connect two extension cords to a central outlet.

■ **Under the sofa.** Add a floor-mounted receptacle under the sofa to keep long lamp cords from running across the floor to the wall. Never run an extension cord under a rug; this is a fire hazard!

■ **Bend the rules.** If you're sure that a table and lamp will be located in one particular spot, consider placing the receptacle behind it a little higher than usual so the cord remains hidden.

HOW BIG SHOULD THE LAMPSHADE BE?

■ **You be the judge.** At one time, hard and fast rules determined the choice of a shade, but these are rapidly being abandoned in favor of utility and personal style preference.

■ **One of the few remaining guidelines:** Look for a shade that hides all mechanical parts, and whose bottom does not extend past the top of the lamp.

■ **Another general suggestion:** The broadest part of the shade should measure two to two and a half times the width of the lamp.

■ **When selecting a new shade,** always take the lamp with you so you can preview how they look together. Try several different shades before making your final choice. The combination should not look top-heavy, yet it should not look too small at the top (lamp shops typically refer to this as a "pinhead lamp"). (See *page 21* for more lampshade ideas.)

■**DESIGN TIP** When a wall-mounted lamp has a cord that must extend several feet to reach the receptacle, cover the cord and keep it vertical with a sleek metal channel made for the purpose. These cord covers, which come in several finishes including one you can paint, are available at most specialty lighting stores.

■ If a lamp cord seems too noticeable against your floor or the carpet, consider rewiring it with another color. Cords come in black, brown, white, ivory, and gold-tone. A lamp-rewiring kit costs only a little more than the cord alone.

DOWNLIGHT SCONCE

UPLIGHT SCONCE

**WALL-MOUNTED
SWING-ARM LAMP
(ADJUSTS VERTICALLY)**

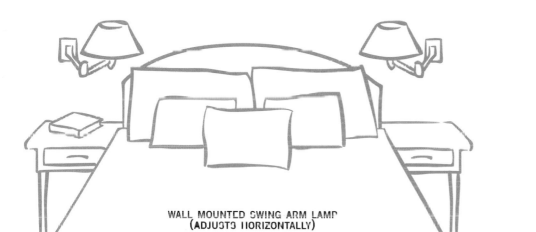

**WALL MOUNTED SWING ARM LAMP
(ADJUSTS HORIZONTALLY)**

DESIGN TIP A dark-colored room requires more light than a light-colored room. If you paint your room a darker color, you may need to change your lamps, adding more translucent lampshades or brighter bulbs to make up the difference.

■ The color of every surface in a room—walls, floor, ceiling, and all the furnishings—either reflects or absorbs light. The color and brightness of the "light" your eye sees is the combined product of the actual light plus its many reflections. Because so much depends on the room itself, try out a new lamp, fitted with the right bulb, in a room before making your final decision to buy.

**SWING-ARM
LAMP**

**MULTISOCKET
LAMP**

**SINGLE-SOCKET
LAMP**

**TORCHÈRE
LAMP**

ROPE LAMP
TIME
1 day
SUPPLIES
- Ginger-jar lamp
- Sandpaper (optional)
- ½"-diameter sisal rope (the lamp in the photo required almost 100 feet)
- Glue gun; hotmelt adhesive
- Parchment shade

PAINT CAN LAMP
TIME
1–2 days
SUPPLIES
- Two new, empty 1-gallon paint cans with lids
- Several colors of latex or acrylic paint
- Small amount of pebbles for weight
- Glue gun; hotmelt adhesive
- White paper shade (or another shade and primed canvas)

A FABULOUS FIBER: ROPE LAMP

Cowboys call it rope, and sailors call it line— whatever word you prefer, wrapping sisal cord around a ho-hum ginger jar is a simple way to create a more contemporary fixture.

Note: Use a continuous length of rope to avoid having to piece it, or piece the rope in numerous places for consistency.

- **If your lamp is very shiny,** scuff it up slightly with sandpaper so the glue sticks better.
- **Beginning at the bottom of the lamp,** apply hot glue and wind the rope in a spiral around the lamp (apply only the amount of glue that you can cover with rope in about a minute; otherwise the glue hardens too soon).
- **Top with a new** parchment shade.

■DESIGN TIP Choose table and floor lamps with heavy bases for maximum stability. If the lamp is hollow, fill it with something that adds weight. Place lamps where you're unlikely to bump them.

■ If you're trying to "baby-proof" your house, consider anchoring lamps to the floor or tabletop temporarily with a small metal strap or angle iron, using screws to attach one end to the underside of the lamp base and the other end into a more stable surface.

A SPLASH OF LIGHT: PAINT CAN LAMP

Satisfy your "inner artist" with the perfect lamp for a studio or crafts room. It's made from empty paint cans and topped with a paper or canvas shade decorated any way you like.

- **Dribble several colors of paint** around the top of each paint can and let dry.
- **Drill ½"-diameter holes in the exact centers** of both lids and the bottom of one can.
- **Fill the undrilled can about one-third full of pebbles;** press both lids on firmly.
- **Follow the instructions for making a lamp on** *page 14,* but stack the cans (with the filled can on the bottom) and glue them together before tightening the washers on the threaded rod. (You do not need a base or cap with this lamp.)
- **Make the shade:** If using a white paper shade, go to the next step. If your shade needs to be covered before you decorate it, make a pattern by rolling the shade over a large sheet of paper and tracing the edges. Cut the pattern ½" larger than the shade all around. Cut the pattern from the canvas and attach the canvas to the shade (glue one straight edge to the seam on the shade; fold the top and bottom edges to the inside of the shade and glue them).
- **Dribble, spatter, or squiggle paint** onto the shade and let dry.

BAMBOO LAMP
TIME
1–2 days
SUPPLIES
- PVC pipe: 12"×3" diameter
- PVC end cap
- 12"-long bamboo pieces
- Wooden base
- Acrylic paint
- Glue gun; hotmelt adhesive
- Length of ½"-wide sisal rope
- Wicker shade

PAINTED LAMP
TIME
1 day
SUPPLIES
- Candlestick lamp
- Masking tape
- 1"-wide brush made for water-base paint
- Water-base primer
- Latex enamel paint
- Black paper shade
- White acrylic paint

NATURAL SELECTION: BAMBOO LAMP
A naturalist's enthusiasm for using plant materials can extend to lighting fixtures, as this handsome bamboo-encased lamp proves.
Note: Buy PVC pipe in the plumbing section of a hardware or home improvement store; many stores will cut it to the required length for you.

- **Glue the end cap to one end** of the PVC pipe.
- **Using the glue gun and hotmelt adhesive,** attach the wooden base to the uncapped bottom of the pipe.
- **Paint the base and the pipe** to match the bamboo, letting it dry completely.
- **Wire the pipe to make a lamp** according to the instructions on *page 14*.
- **Glue the bamboo pieces all around the PVC pipe,** covering it completely.
- **Wrap the center of the lamp with sisal rope** as many times as desired; knot the rope and trim the ends.
- **Top the lamp with a wicker shade.**

TOTAL MAKEOVER: PAINTED LAMP
Use paint to add a designer's touch to an otherwise ordinary fixture. Consider changing the color of your lamp or painting bold stripes on its shade to coordinate with other furnishings or simply update it for more pizzazz.

- **Use masking tape** to tape off all areas of the lamp, including the electrical cord, that you don't want to paint.
- **Apply one or two coats of primer;** let dry.
- **Apply one or more coats of latex enamel,** allowing each coat to dry completely before applying the next. Remove the masking tape.
- **Measure 12 equal sections along the top edge** of the shade, marking lightly with a pencil. Beginning directly below one of the marks, repeat the process, marking equal sections around the bottom edge.
- **Using the marks as guides,** paint freehand lines from top to bottom and fill in alternate sections with the white paint.
- **Top the lamp with the painted shade.**

■**DESIGN TIP** Come home to rooms that are cheerfully lit instead of dark and unwelcoming. Plug at least one lamp into a clock timer in a receptacle. Program the timer to turn on right before you come home and to go off a few hours later. This is an inexpensive way to make your home more safe and secure too.

FLOWERPOT LAMP

TIME

1–2 days

SUPPLIES

- 10" terra-cotta pot
- Plywood round to fit inside pot
- Primer; latex paint
- Paintbrushes
- Four 6"×¼"-diameter dowels
- Glue gun; hotmelt adhesive
- Paper shade
- Ball-shape finial

BLOCK LAMP

TIME

1–2 days

SUPPLIES

- Wooden box
- Unfinished wood tiles (1¼"×1¼"×⅛")
- Wood glue
- Unfinished wood base to fit lamp
- Black paste wax; soft cloth
- Black paper shade

UPDATED FAVORITE: FLOWERPOT LAMP

Looking like a throwback to the era of disco and happy faces, this retro-'70s lamp has a striped-flowerpot base and a flower-power shade.

- **Prime the plywood round** and the paper shade.
- **Paint the plywood round green.**
- **Along the top edge of the pot,** measure 12 equal sections, marking lightly with a pencil. Beginning directly below one of the marks, repeat the process, marking 12 equal sections around the bottom.
- **Using the marks as guides, paint freehand lines** from top to bottom and fill in alternate sections with two colors of paint; pink and orange were used here. Continue the colors on the top 3 inches inside the pot.
- **Paint the shade yellow** or another light color.
- **Paint large '70s-style flowers on the shade** as shown, using pink, orange, or other colors.
- **Glue the plywood round inside the pot.**
- **Wire the pot to make a lamp** as instructed on *page 14,* leaving at least 6 inches of the center rod (between the plywood and the socket) clear.
- **Glue four ¼-inch-diameter dowels** all around the rod.
- **Paint the center rod and dowels green;** let dry.
- **Place the shade on the lamp,** securing it a ball-shape finial.

WOOD-GRAIN SOPHISTICATE: BLOCK LAMP

Elegant in its simplicity yet complex with its multitoned wood grains, this small lamp has a black shade that throws most of the light downward, making it ideal for areas where mood lighting is important.

- **Remove any hardware from the box** (the base in the photo is a double recipe box from a crafts supply store), and glue the pieces together.
- **Apply wood glue to the back of each wooden tile** and cover the box completely (if necessary, use a small saw to trim the tiles to fit).
- **Glue on the wooden base.**
- **Wire the box to make a lamp** according to the instructions on *page 14.*
- **Using the cloth as an applicator,** apply black paste wax to the wooden blocks and base, buffing the wax to a sheen when it dries. The wax makes the end grains of the wood take on slightly different tones.
- **Top the lamp with a black paper shade.**

▪**DESIGN TIP** Hiding table lamp cords can be a challenge. Running the cord straight back and down a leg is usually the best solution. Although it's best not to have a cord that is so long that it poses a safety hazard, don't worry if a cord shows a bit.

PAPER LAMP

TIME

1–2 days

SUPPLIES

- Old torchère-type floor lamp
- Cylindrical wire lampshade frame with central ring that surrounds the lightbulb
- Wire cutters
- White rice paper (from an art or crafts supply store)
- White glue

SHINING TOWER: PAPER LAMP

Create a dramatic column of light by making a rice-paper "slipcover" for an old floor lamp.

- **Cut away the vertical wires** from the lampshade and discard them. You will only use the two circular rings at the top and bottom.
- **Measure from the top of the lightbulb** to 2" above the base of the lamp; measure the circumference of the top ring. Add 1" to each measurement to obtain the dimensions of the rice paper.
- **Make a large piece of rice paper** by gluing together several smaller sheets (overlap the edges about ¼", joining them with a thin line of glue).
- **Beginning at the top edge, glue** the large piece of paper to the wire frame by turning the edges ½" to the inside and attaching with white glue.
- **Glue the back seam together;** attach the bottom edge to the bottom frame as in the previous step.
- **Handling the paper shade gently, crumple** the paper from top to bottom to create texture.
- **Stretch the shade,** gently smoothing out the wrinkles, and attach it to the lamp.

■**DESIGN TIP** If you're fond of your lamp but it's the wrong height, you can fix the problem in many ways. Change the harp to another size, replace the lampshade with one more suitable, take off the base, add a taller base, or remove or add spacers between the base and the socket. Or you can raise your lamp on a stylish platform of stacked art books.

ALTERED PERSONALITY: CHANGING THE SHADE

- **Your selection of a lampshade** sometimes makes all the difference in whether a lamp works for a particular location. When choosing a shade for a lamp, consider its function, shape, color, size, and the style of the room. If possible, echo the shape of the base with your shade, and if you like, repeat its color, material, or general theme.
- **To channel the light downward** or to highlight a tabletop collection, *above,* choose an opaque shade. A dark shade lined with gold-tone foil casts a warmer light, no matter what type of bulb you use (also see *page 73*). For even light throughout the room, *below,* opt for a translucent fabric shade in white, beige, or cream.

overhead
fixtures

Carefully chosen ceiling fixtures—often some of the most noticeable details in your home—should function well and highlight the style of your room.

overheadfixtures

Ceiling fixtures are like the jewelry of a home, sparkling with light, drawing the eye, and attesting to your good taste. There's more than meets the eye, though, to selecting the right fixture for every room. And often, it's not one central lighting source but a combination of several that is the right solution. For example, on *pages 22–23,* several spotlights accent the staircase and vaulted ceiling, a sconce lights the art and balcony, and an oversize opening frames a view of the gleaming fixture in the dining room. On these pages, observe how various sources work together to create interesting lighting. *Clockwise from upper left:*

● In a light-flooded entry, a fanlight, sidelights, and a glass door suffice in the daytime but, at night, a pendant light provides a traditional touch. A recessed downlight defines the cross-hall.

● A Craftsman-style fixture, hung high above for general illumination, echoes the distinctive windows and other architectural elements. Recessed downlights and sconces provide additional light.

● Glass pendant fixtures, braced with an eye-catching cable support system, illuminate the room. Skylights and a sconce near the peak further accent the angular vaulted ceiling.

● While swing-arm lamps focus reading light at the head of the bed, the main illumination in this lofty room comes from a pair of wall sconces shining from high above.

● A lighted ceiling fan partnered with a similarly shaped translucent glass fixture casts an even light throughout the seating area. Recessed downlights highlight the fireplace wall.

● Halogen lights mounted on a track focus directly on the floor-to-ceiling wall of art. The halogen bulbs produce an extremely white light that doesn't distort the artwork's colors.

Functional lighting installed in the ceiling over a dining or breakfast table is essential because many activities, from eating to doing homework, take place there. *Clockwise from upper left:*

● Inconspicuous halogen pendants focus bright light on the table at night, but skylights supply most of the light in the daytime.

● Three recessed fixtures spread pools of golden light over the table, which can be repositioned for parties, if necessary, because there's no chandelier to work around.

● Suspended from two tautly stretched parallel wires, low-voltage halogen fixtures offer a lighthearted way to light a peninsula. As with track lights, you can position halogens anywhere on the wires.

● Graceful wrought-iron curves in the chandelier echo the tapestry design, reinforcing the impact of both. The tall light-socket extensions and flame-shape bulbs resemble real candles.

● A pendant fixture casts diffused light through translucent glass with metal vine accents, and also bounces it from the ceiling. Supplemental recessed lights brighten the four corners of the room.

● Form definitely equals function in the case of these glass pendants, which hang a comfortable distance (about 30 inches) above a trestle table in the massively braced dining area.

● White-painted Craftsman-style fixtures harmonize with the crisp white trim of a turn-of-the-century-style home. Darker fixtures would appear too heavy, given the color scheme of the room.

Overhead fixtures set the tone for the room with attention-grabbing features or retire into the ceiling to do their job less visibly but no less importantly. *Clockwise from upper left:*

● Recessed fixtures illuminate the room for general purposes, while industrial-style pendants bring task lighting to the island.

● It's hard to say how many fixtures are too many when all do their part to provide even lighting in the kitchen. A combination of suspended halogen lights and recessed spotlights works well.

● One main ceiling fixture may be enough in a small kitchen—but only if it's supplemented by lighting elsewhere in the room. Few rooms get adequate illumination from a single light source.

● There's safety in numbers when fixtures hang over counters where they do the most good. The black metal pendants have reflective white linings that aim light downward.

● Inconspicuous does not mean ineffective. Recessed canister lights with reflectors or special trims, installed in a grid for a uniform lighting pattern, often provide the most light for the money.

● A heavy iron fixture has "candles" that echo the kitchen's baronial style, but it also has a downlight to illuminate the counter. Recessed lights brighten corners in the potentially dark room.

● Blue-and-white shades top off country-casual pendants and the combination pot rack/chandelier. Frosted bulbs diffuse their glow, which is supplemented by general lighting from recessed fixtures.

overheadfixtures ideas & projects

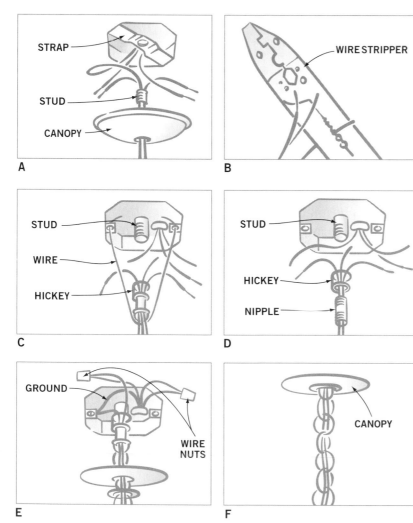

A

STRAP

STUD

CANOPY

B

WIRE STRIPPER

C

STUD

WIRE

HICKEY

D

STUD

HICKEY

NIPPLE

E

GROUND

WIRE NUTS

F

CANOPY

REPLACING A CEILING FIXTURE

Most novices can replace a ceiling fixture with one of the same general type in about 30 minutes.

■ **You need:** voltage meter, screwdriver, wire stripper, needle-nose pliers, wire nuts, ladder.

1. Before beginning, turn off the power at the main control box. Use the voltage meter to make sure that no power flows through the fixture.

2. Disconnect the old fixture. Examine how it was attached—some fixtures are secured with bolts to a metal strap (see A), and others have a hickey mounted to a stud at the center of the box (see C). If the new and old fixtures are different types, make sure you have all necessary parts.

3. Strap mounting works best with lightweight fixtures. You can usually reuse the old strap. Use the wire stripper to strip ¾ inch of insulation from the leads on the new fixture (see B). If they are strand-type wires, twist the bare ends slightly.

4. Stud-and-hickey mountings support heavier fixtures. To temporarily support the new fixture while you work, hang it with coat-hanger wire from the ceiling mount (see C). Screw a nipple into the hickey; wires exit through the side of the hickey (see D).

5. Thread the hickey onto the stud, or screw the bolt into the strap to mechanically secure the light fixture.

6. Connect matching wires by twisting wire nuts around the ends (see E), and gently push the wires up inside the box. Turn on the power. If the fixture lights, the connection is good. Turn off the power again; raise and secure the canopy (see F).

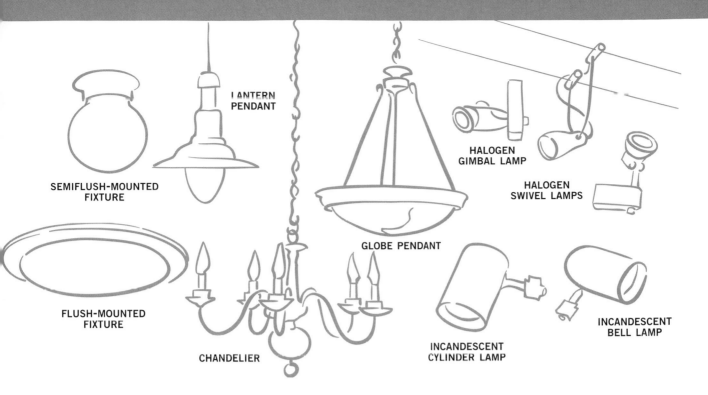

SEMIFLUSH-MOUNTED FIXTURE

LANTERN PENDANT

HALOGEN GIMBAL LAMP

HALOGEN SWIVEL LAMPS

FLUSH-MOUNTED FIXTURE

GLOBE PENDANT

CHANDELIER

INCANDESCENT CYLINDER LAMP

INCANDESCENT BELL LAMP

OVERHEAD-FIXTURE BASICS

How large? How high? How far apart? Use these guidelines to clear up the mystery in choosing ceiling light fixtures for any room in your home:

■ **When selecting a chandelier, size matters as much as style.** A fixture that's too big overpowers the room, while a too-small chandelier seems out of proportion with the space. A good approach is to measure the width and length of the dining room in feet. Add the two numbers. The sum should be the diameter of the chandelier in inches. For example: A 12×14-foot dining room requires a chandelier approximately 26 inches in diameter. A 10×12-foot room needs a fixture about 22 inches across.

■ **The bottom of a hanging fixture is typically at least 7 feet above the floor** to provide adequate head clearance in traffic areas.

■ **Lowering a fixture from the ceiling makes lighting more efficient** because the light doesn't have to travel as far. Try to choose a pendant or another hanging fixture for use with very high ceilings. Exposed trusses and beams offer other mounting opportunities below the ceiling.

■ **If the fixture hangs over a dining table,** the bottom of the fixture should hang about 30 inches above the table in a room with an 8-foot ceiling. For every additional foot of ceiling height, raise the fixture an extra 1 to 3 inches.

■ **Extra-tall ceilings sometimes present special challenges.** Buy additional matching chain or a longer down rod when you buy your light fixture;

have a competent electrician extend the wiring.

■ **Light from a recessed fixture spreads out in a cone-shape pattern.** The farther away the light is, the bigger the area it covers and the more brightness it loses as it spreads out. Change from a floodlight bulb to a spotlight bulb for more intensity, or change the route the light takes by installing a different trim.

■ **Most recessed fixtures are installed in a grid.** You can set the fixtures as far apart as the room is high, but it's usually better if they are closer so their patterns of light overlap. The closer they are to the wall, the brighter (and higher up) they illuminate it, as the plane of the wall intersects the cone of light.

■ **Fluorescent fixtures are best used** in the kitchen or workshop for even lighting, or for accent lighting, such as cove lighting, in other rooms. Avoid using them in a dining area because the color of most bulbs makes food look less appetizing. For more information on special effects using fluorescent lighting, see *page 43*.

■**DESIGN TIP** After a track is installed, you can use several types of housings along its length for different purposes. Choose fixtures of the same color and same general shape from the manufacturer who made the track. You also can mix different types of bulbs to illuminate various features, even if the housings are all the same.

■ Use track lighting to turn a dark hallway into an art gallery.

PICK A PERIOD

Should you buy new fixtures for an older house? What if you find a chandelier you love in an antiques store? Will it look out of place in a more contemporary location?

One guideline is to choose fixtures in a style from the same time period or later than the architectural style of the house. Fixtures from an earlier time period often make the home look outdated. For example, a colonial-style house looks fine with hand-wrought tin fixtures or a multiarm brass and glass chandelier. But don't furnish a sleek, big-city dining room with a Western wagon wheel fixture fitted with hob-nail milk-glass shades!

BITTERSWEET WREATH

TIME

1–2 hours

SUPPLIES

- Small, straight tree branches, 18–24" long
- Florist's wire
- Several strings of miniature lights (with brown or green wire)
- Fresh bittersweet vines
- Heavy-duty nylon fishing line (optional)
- 1–2"-wide brass ring (optional)
- Ceiling hook (optional)
- White extension cord

DECORATIVE SHADES

TIME

5 minutes to 1 day

SUPPLIES

- Existing fixture
- Paper shades
- Paint, paintbrushes, rubber stamps, trims, braids, glue gun, hotmelt adhesive

NATURE'S CHOICE: BITTERSWEET WREATH

Hang a bittersweet wreath from an ordinary fixture to create a sophisticated accent with a touch of wild (and delightful) abandon.

Note: Fresh, pliable bittersweet vines are available from many florists in the fall. The berries are poisonous if consumed, so exercise caution around children or pets.

- **Place tree branches with corners overlapping** to form a rectangular frame in the desired size; wire the corners together with florist's wire. Reinforce the branches with an X of branches in the center, wiring it as before.

- **Wind a string of lights loosely** around the frame. Gently wrap bittersweet vines and more strings of lights, with plugs joined, around the frame; tuck in the vines to secure them as necessary, but avoid wrapping them too tightly.

- **Attach the vine wreath** to the bottom of an existing chandelier with nylon fishing line or twist ties, if desired. Or, to hang the wreath by itself, tie a length of nylon fishing line to each of the four corners, joining all four at the center by tying them to a small brass ring. Hang the ring on a ceiling hook.

- **Plug the wreath into an extension cord** that leads to an outlet.

LITTLE EXTRAS: DECORATIVE SHADES

A painted or printed shade is one of those custom details that distinguishes ordinary fixtures from those that have that certain something. Consider changing a plain shade (or shades) in one of the following ways to add a decorator touch to a fixture you may already own.

- **If painting your shade, simplify a design** from fabric or wallpaper used elsewhere in the room, or choose small geometrics or a striped pattern. Adapt the instructions on *page 19* to paint a striped shade.

- **Use rubber stamps and ink or paint to add simple, repetitive motifs to the shade.** Rubber stamps are available in hundreds of designs.

- **Glue beaded fringe or woven braid** to the bottom of a standard shade; look for these trims in fabric or crafts stores.

- **Check lamp shops' selection** of printed and specialty-paper shades. They usually have animal-print, marbleized, holiday, or novelty shades that add instant flair to your lighting. You can switch shades quickly, easily, and inexpensively to suit your mood or the occasion.

■DESIGN TIP Clip-on shades offer a stylish way to reduce the glare of bare chandelier bulbs, but keeping them positioned straight on the bulbs may try your patience. You may find that they fit better on a slightly wider lightbulb.

RAFFIA-WRAP CHANDELIER

TIME
1–2 days

SUPPLIES
- Inexpensive metal chandelier
- Spray paint to match raffia
- Raffia (available at crafts stores)
- Glue gun; hotmelt adhesive
- Paper shades
- Tracing paper
- Grass-cloth wallcovering
- Spray adhesive
- Cardboard

NEW ATTITUDE: RAFFIA-WRAP CHANDELIER

Instead of discarding a worn or outdated fixture, transform it into a designer's dream by wrapping it in raffia, complete with sassy tassels.

- **Spray the chandelier with paint;** dry thoroughly.
- **Beginning at the top of each arm** and working quickly, apply several beads of glue at a time and wrap with raffia. To wrap the center portion of the chandelier, twist together about eight strands of raffia and glue as before.
- **Draw a pattern of the shade by rolling it on paper,** tracing along the edges as you go. Using the pattern (and always aligning it the same way), cut a piece of grass-cloth wallcovering for each shade. Working with one piece at a time, spray the back of the grass cloth, align one straight edge with the seam, and press the grass cloth firmly to the shade.
- **Repeat to cover the other shades.** If desired, trim the edges of the shade by gluing on twists of raffia.

TASSELS (Make one for each arm of the fixture.)
- **Cut a piece of cardboard** about 4 inches wide. Place a length of raffia along one edge and wrap the cardboard with raffia.
- **Tie the length together to hold the loops tightly;** cut the bottom loops. Wrap another length of raffia around the top of the tassel, securing the ends with hotmelt adhesive.
- **Tie each tassel to the chandelier** with the loose ends of the raffia, and trim any remaining ends.

■DESIGN TIP Sometimes the canopy on a new fixture is slightly too small to cover the old hole in the ceiling. You can buy a decorative medallion in the size you need at most lighting or home improvement stores. Paint the medallion to match the ceiling or give it a decorative paint treatment; install it as directed by the manufacturer. Then install the fixture (see instructions on *page 30*).

special effects

Accent lighting draws the eye much like a magnet. Use it to emphasize a display, set a mood, or create a focal point in an otherwise dark area.

specialeffects

Often overlooked during the planning stage, low-voltage accent lights and wall-mounted sconces that illuminate specific areas can make a dazzling difference in a room. If accurate color is important, consider using halogen bulbs (used in many of the fixtures shown here). Available in both standard and low-voltage, these offer crisper, whiter light than incandescent bulbs. Observe how simple ideas add utility and drama to a variety of spaces.
Clockwise from upper left:

● Sconces mounted high on the walls define the raised beam ceiling of this family room. These decorative fixtures not only provide general illumination, they also accent art that hangs near the ceiling.

● Picture lights that illuminate artwork have slim bulbs hidden behind a metal housing. Mounted on the wall or attached to the painting's frame, they usually plug into a wall outlet. Choose a fixture at least half the width of the painting for best illumination.

● Flanking the entrance to the family room, sconces installed above eye level provide light for the hallway. A dimmer switch easily adjusts them to lower levels for safety at night.

● Natural light pours through the glass-door cabinets, supplementing the sleek pendant lights above the counter.

● Above the mantel, sconces create a focal point, highlighting the above-eye-level Craftsman-style molding. A matching sconce above the windows emphasizes the room's high ceiling.

● Four 10-inch-deep niches above the fireplace provide enough depth for books or a display of favorite objects. Although all are equipped with tiny halogen lights, the bottom two are turned off, shifting the emphasis to the objects above.

Seldom-noticed features gain prominence with special-effect lighting. *Clockwise from upper left:*

A wooden cornice more than a foot below the ceiling provides a channel for both cove lighting and recessed downlights. The cove lights are spaced to create a pattern of light on the wall and ceiling.

Rather than wasting space at the end of an island, box it in to create a shallow display niche with a recessed light in the top. Most kitchen islands are wired for electrical outlets, so adding a light and switch is usually easy.

A downlight in the arched recess illuminates a built-in storage cabinet, creating an attractive display or serving area. The lights aimed toward the ceiling set the mood.

Glass shelves in both the kitchen cabinet and the display niche allow light to flow through, highlighting items below. To minimize shadows, position lights slightly toward the fronts of shelves.

Formerly wasted wall space displays favorite bottles lit from above by a halogen spotlight. This spotlight and unusual frosted sconces beside the mirror have separate dimmer switches.

Simple birch-plywood boxes screwed into the side cabinets span the sink without blocking light from ceiling fixtures mounted farther out. Additional recessed ceiling lights illuminate the display.

Puck-style halogen spotlights accent crystal in the top cabinets; slim-line undercounter halogens evenly light the mirror-backed bar.

Other areas of the house, even those less public, also benefit from special-effect lighting. *Clockwise from upper left:*

● High-tech halogen sconces for reading free up space on the bedside tables, while a fixture mounted above a floating open frame bounces light off the ceiling and down toward the bed.

● Slim fluorescent fixtures mounted behind a tile-covered plywood shadow-box panel create a dramatic show of light against the terra-cotta wall.

● Bare-bulb lighting has long been the choice in theater dressing rooms and is just as useful for shadow-free lighting above a vanity. Mirrors multiply the available light.

● Tucked into a dormer with halogen lighting above, this vanity dispenses with the usual mirrored wall in favor of a small, light-ringed mirror for shaving or putting on makeup.

● A canister-shape uplight creates a dance of light and dark by causing the display stand to throw a pattern of shadows on the wall. This is an excellent way to enliven a dark corner.

● Use large, sculptural plants and backlighting to create a silhouette effect, or throw a shadow on the wall with an uplight. Both are particularly dramatic when paired with a rich wall color.

● When you're entertaining informally, whimsical items add to the party mood. Even a simple string of lights draped over a curtain rod can make a casual gathering of friends seem like a celebration.

specialeffects ideas & projects

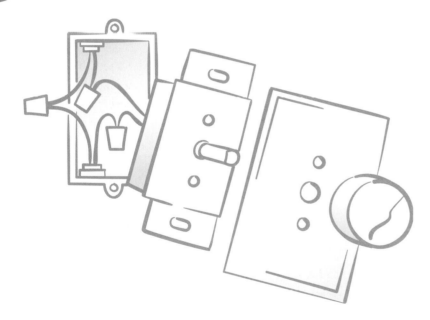

A GOOD INVESTMENT: THE DIMMER SWITCH

Of all the things you can do to improve your lighting and create special effects, adding dimmer switches is among the most useful. A dimmer switch, also called a rheostat, is sold in home improvement stores and is extremely easy to install. It costs only a few dollars and can help save money on future electric bills by using fewer watts. In addition, this tiny piece of equipment has other, more subtle, advantages. It has the ability to completely transform the tone of the lighting—from a too-bright blare to a gentle conversational murmur or a soft, romantic whisper.

INSTALLING A ROTARY DIMMER SWITCH

■ **Use an incandescent dimmer only for an incandescent light, not a fluorescent light.** Special dimmers are available for fluorescents.

■ **These instructions apply only to two-way rotary dimmer switches.** (You can also install slider-type switches with the following method.) If your fixture is controlled by only one switch, be sure to buy a two-way dimmer. If more than one switch turns it on and off, you need a three-way dimmer, which is a bit more complicated to install.

■ **You'll need a dimmer switch, screwdriver, volt meter, wire stripper, and wire nuts.** Wire nuts are often included with the dimmer.

1. **Turn off the power at the main panel.** Unscrew and remove the switchplate. Test the current to make sure it's off. Loosen the terminal screws on the light switch; remove the wires. Set the light switch aside. Trim and re-strip the wires.

2. **Attach the dimmer switch.** Connect the wires, as shown *left,* by twisting a wire nut around the ends of each two matching wires.

3. **Space will be tight,** but tuck the connected wires inside the box, attaching the dimmer switch with the screws provided. Replace the switch cover; put the rotary dial on the spindle.

■**DESIGN TIP** Install a dimmer switch in the bath or hallway. You can turn the lights down when asleep, providing a safe path if you get up during the night.

FLUORESCENT LIGHTING

Throughout this book, you see a number of instances in which rooms have cove lighting, valance lighting, or cornice lighting. In most cases, the light comes from fluorescent tubes mounted behind a wooden support that hides the bulb from view.

■ **Fluorescent lights are the workhorses of the lighting world,** providing more light at less cost than either incandescent or halogen bulbs. They come in many lengths, shapes, and even colors.

■ **Consider switching the bulb** in a standard lamp to one of the new fluorescent bulbs with a screw-in base. The initial cost is greater, but they will soon pay for themselves in reduced costs.

■ **The color of light is always important** but never more so than in fluorescent bulbs. Typically stores and offices use "cool white" fluorescent bulbs for cost efficiency, but many find these objectionable in their own home. Instead choose full-spectrum bulbs to approximate sunlight or "warm white" bulbs that more closely resemble incandescent light.

FLUORESCENT SPECIAL EFFECTS

■ **Cornice lighting:** Dramatize draperies or shine a soft light downward by mounting fluorescent

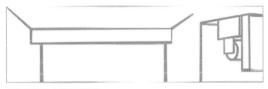

CORNICE LIGHTING

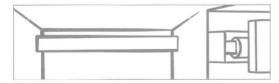

VALANCE LIGHTING

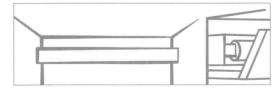

COVE LIGHTING

UNDERCABINET LIGHTING

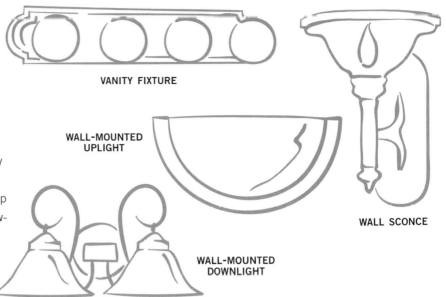

VANITY FIXTURE

WALL-MOUNTED UPLIGHT

WALL-MOUNTED DOWNLIGHT

WALL SCONCE

bulbs under a cornice. Build the cornice with 1×2 and 1×6 lumber; install the tube 6 inches from the wall and mount the cornice with large angle brackets.

■ **Valance lighting:** This light shines both upward and downward to wash both wall and ceiling with light. Use 1×2 and 1×6 lumber and angle brackets. Or attach translucent plastic on the top to create a lighted display shelf.

■ **Cove lighting:** Highlight a ceiling, outline a room, or accent a special feature. Build a channel from lumber and angle brackets, paint the inside surface with white paint for better reflective qualities, and mount the bulb about 1 foot below the ceiling (in most cases).

■ **Undercabinet lighting:** This task lighting installed directly over a work surface is especially important in a kitchen or workshop. Install fixtures near the front, not the rear, of the cabinet where they will be hidden by the skirt. Ideally, at least two-thirds of the length of the undercabinet area should be lighted.

■**DESIGN TIP** For best coverage, choose the longest fluorescent bulbs that fit the available space.
■ For undercabinet lighting, you may opt to use individual low-voltage halogen fixtures instead of continuous fluorescent strips. If so, install the light 12 inches on center. Never use halogen bulbs in places where they could come in contact with your hands, fabric, or flammable materials; they often reach very high temperatures.

SPECIALTY BULBS

Buying a "regular" incandescent lightbulb for a lamp or ceiling fixture isn't nearly as easy as it used to be. Now, in addition to its wattage and base size, you can consider these variations: standard, torpedo, globe, clear, frosted, chrome/mirror, faceted, three-way, flickering flame, spot, reflector, flood, enriched, amber, pale-pink, long-life, full-spectrum, plant-growing, low-voltage, vibration-resistant, insect-repelling, and many others. You may even discover that you can adapt your old fixture to fit your needs—simply by changing the bulb.

LIGHT TABLES
TIME
5 minutes
SUPPLIES
- Canvas-lined laundry hamper or wicker hamper
- Small lamp with a narrow translucent shade
- Glass cut to fit the top of the hamper (optional)

BASKET LIGHT
TIME
5 minutes
SUPPLIES
- Two matching baskets without handles
- Several strings of clear indoor/outdoor lights

UNHAMPERED BY TRADITION: LIGHT TABLES
- **Create a stable base** in the hamper bottom. Level the legs, if necessary, or reinforce the bottom by inserting a piece of plywood.
- **When using a canvas-lined laundry hamper** *above left,* place an old table lamp inside and rest a new piece of glass on top to create a stunning table that emits a gentle glow.
- **When using a wicker hamper** *below,* place a lamp inside, taking care that the bulb is at least 6 inches from the top. The container essentially becomes an allover lampshade. With light peeking out through openings in the weave, the lamp provides unobtrusive lighting for conversation or television watching.

A TISKIT, A TASKET: BASKET LIGHT
- **Take two baskets, a few strings of clear holiday lights,** and voilà—you have a unique side table *above right* that casts a pattern of light onto the wall and floor. With intricate shafts of light shining through the wicker, this basket light also makes an unusual plant stand.
- **Crumple several strings of indoor/outdoor minilights loosely into** one basket and lay the cord over the edge before plugging them in. Top with an identical basket. As with any string of lights, these should not be left unattended.
- **Experiment with light patterns** by varying the distance between the baskets and the wall—the closer they are, the more pronounced the design.
- **Connect several baskets** of different heights and shapes together with florist's wire or twist ties to create an interesting sculpture of light and form.

LIGHTED CHAIRS
TIME
15 minutes
SUPPLIES
- Wicker chairs with metal frames
- One string of flexible plastic-tube lights per chair
- Twist ties

PAPER LANTERN
TIME
5 minutes
SUPPLIES
- Light kit made for a paper lantern
- One purchased paper lantern
- One incandescent lightbulb: 25–40 watts

GUESTS OF HONOR: LIGHTED CHAIRS

- **All eyes go to these chairs** rimmed with tiny bulbs *above*, a striking effect that is simple to duplicate with flexible plastic-tube lights. Although this type of tube lighting was once used primarily to line traffic paths in commercial installations such as movie theaters, the lights are now widely available in several different colors and lengths for holiday decorating.
- **Edge the underside of each wicker chair** with a standard tube of white lights, secured (but not too tightly) by twist ties wrapped around the metal frame.

DESIGN TIP For memorable party decorations, consider replacing removable shades on pendant light fixtures with paper lanterns (whether you can do it depends on the style of your fixtures). Then, to continue the theme, hang paper lanterns throughout the room and in the trees outside.

GENTLE CELEBRATION: PAPER LANTERN

- **Many import shops offer paper lanterns** in both traditional moon white and breezy, colored designs. They are especially charming on a covered or enclosed porch *above* that's decorated with an Asian or a garden theme.
- **These lanterns cover and soften the effect** of bare electric bulbs (or even a string of bulbs). Often the shops offer lamp-hanging kits made specifically for the lanterns they sell.
- **Hang the fixture first.** Attach the cord to the ceiling with a hook (or hooks) so the bulb is at the desired level.
- **Examine the lantern.** Many lanterns have a wire armature at the top with a round hole to accommodate the lightbulb. Carefully insert the socket of the fixture through the top of the round hole, then screw in the lightbulb from the bottom of the lantern to hold it in place. Check for adequate clearance between the bulb and the lantern.

ACCENT LIGHT
TIME
2 minutes
SUPPLIES
- Medium or large
plant with attractive
branch structure
- Clip-on or can-type
plant light

TINY WHITE LIGHTS
TIME
15 minutes
SUPPLIES
- Large, leafy plant
- Clear indoor/outdoor
strings of lights

NATURE AT NIGHT: ACCENT LIGHT

- **Add instant drama to rooms at night** by bathing favorite plants in a warm glow of light. Choose tiny directional lights that clip onto branches or larger can-type plant lights that channel the beams upward *above*.
- **Can-type lights come in several** colors and sizes for use with both large and medium plants. Aimed correctly, they give a plant an almost sculptural quality. Look for these lights in lighting stores, hardware and home improvement stores, or well-stocked garden shops.
- **Even if you're not using lights** specifically made for this purpose, you can emphasize indoor plants in plenty of other ways. Highlight glossy green foliage by aiming a directional floor lamp at the plant (but not so close that you risk scorching the leaves). Or place a small lamp on the floor behind the plant to create backlighting for an interesting branch structure.

FANCY PLANTS: TINY WHITE LIGHTS

- **Another way to add interest** to darkened rooms is to tuck sparkling white lights into the branches of an indoor tree, such as the ficus.
- **Trees with white lights are delightful additions** to decks and other outdoor areas as well, adding flickering, firefly romance to outdoor entertaining.

■ DESIGN TIP To create a fresh and colorful "minigreenhouse" for the dining room or kitchen, remove the door from an armoire or upright cabinet. Fit it with a full-size mirror in the back, add brackets and glass shelves, and install a fluorescent grow-light in the top. (Grow-lights are available at most hardware or home improvement stores.) Fill the cabinet with blooming plants that do well in moderate light—African violets and begonias, for instance. Periodically rotate all plants to the top shelf for even growth.

LIGHT-IN-A-VASE
TIME
2 minutes
SUPPLIES
- Small, battery-powered push light (made for a closet)
- Glass vase with opening wide enough to accommodate the push light and your hand
- Batteries

FOR SPECIAL SPOTS: LIGHT-IN-A-VASE

- **You need to exercise extra creativity** when there's a spot in need of a light but no electrical outlet nearby, as is the case in some hallways or in homes with older wiring. The lamp *above* is actually a wide-top vase. Push down on the light inside and a soft glow immediately fills the dark corner or the hallway, perhaps to guide the way to the switchplate across the room.

- **Making the lamp couldn't be simpler:** Just install the batteries in the back of the push light and place the light in the bottom of the vase. When you need a bit of light, reach your hand inside the vase, press gently, and the light comes on. Press again, and the light goes off.

■**DESIGN TIP** If you'd love to enjoy the warm glow of a fire without the bother of lighting one, put candles in your fireplace instead. Many stores sell multitiered candleholders for pillar or votive candles—simply set them in the fireplace and light them whenever you like. For an even more polished appearance, surround the base of the candleholder with a scattering of shiny river rocks or glass marbles.

PARTY LIGHTS: TABLETOP CANDLES

- **Special-effect lighting sometimes involves no fixture at all.** For those times when a flicker of candlelight is all you need, consider some ways this lovely, low-tech lighting can maximize the mood.

- **For a centerpiece** suitable for a dinner party, a bridal event, or a romantic dinner for two, display candles on a framed mirror *above,* doubling their impact. Use mismatched crystal as containers for flowers and a variety of matching candles, including some that float.

- **For an foyer table** that announces a celebration the moment guests arrive, arrange an assemblage of candles in colors that echo the party's theme or accents used in your home.

entries

Let your entry set the mood for what's to be found deeper within your home. Use light to accent favorite pieces of art, visually expand the space, lead the eye, and make your guests feel at home.

entries

WELCOMING WITH LIGHT. An entry is the first room encountered when arriving, and the last when departing. The correct lighting makes it as beautiful as the rest of your home.

The spacious entry on *pages 48–49* receives enough light from one overhead halogen fixture (wired to a dimmer) that it requires no additional lighting. Suspended from a coffer, the fixture bounces light off the ceiling and also shines through the frosted glass that hides the bulb.

Although flooded with natural light from a skylight and a glass-paned door, the entry *right* also boasts a chandelier and an impressively scaled table lamp. Multiple sources of light allow flexibility, softening the transition between bright sunlight or darkness and the vibrant interior. A subtle interplay exists between the light fixtures and other decorative elements: The entry lamp echoes the columned openings between the two rooms; the brass chandelier matches the switchplate; and the blue flowers on the living room lampshade match the color of the sofa.

DESIGN TIP Repeat motifs, shapes, colors, or materials in lighting fixtures and other elements in the room for more decorative impact.

Choosing the right paint makes a big difference in how well a fixture performs; dark colors absorb light, and light colors reflect it. Look for extra-reflective paints that maximize the light by means of tiny crystals.

LIGHT TO ENHANCE YOUR HOME. The lighting you choose for the entrance hall, which often has little furniture, does a great deal to set the stage for what's to come in the rest of your home. Whether sleek and contemporary, or so old-world traditional that it could have graced a European manor house, you'll find abundant choices in fixtures to exactly suit your style.

● In the contemporary entry *left,* track lighting fixtures provide flexible lighting right where it is needed. Instead of sliding on a track, each fixture is mounted individually to fittings called mono-points. Although this type of installation does not allow for movement, it does permit you to mount a track lighting fixture anywhere that you can install an electrical box. As with other track lighting, you need to use a compatible mono-point made by the same manufacturer.

● Elegant and symmetrical, the focal point of the entry *above* is a traditional chandelier that sets the tone. Two matching table lamps in the stair hall flank the painting, giving the piece additional prominence; the translucent shades let diffused light flow onto the canvas.

A lantern fixture with three delicate electric candles is the primary source of light in the two-story entry *above*, illuminating the stairway as well. Above the door, a picture light casts a glow on art displayed high on the wall; without this light, the art would be in shadows.

Use lighting to enhance important architectural elements. In the Craftsman-style entry *left* a pair of sconces, recessed into niches, illuminates the deep archway between foyer and dining room. Lined with a gold finish, the niches both reflect and warm the light.

DESIGN TIP Create a shallow display niche by recessing a cabinet with a ¼-inch plywood backing between the studs. The niche provides about 3⅜ inches of depth in a standard wall. Wire for a tiny halogen spotlight at the top, and trim the edges with molding.

A NATURAL RESOURCE. Abundant light that floods into an entry through windows or a transom and the door's sidelights is a major asset. Most homes, however, must rely on fixtures to do the job. Ideally these fixtures provide a lovely focal point for overall lighting, using additional lights, if necessary, to banish dark corners.

The two-story entrance hall *above* is a prime example of a room that probably doesn't need much additional light during the day. Nevertheless the desk tucked into the corner benefits from the accent lamp that highlights the painting *above*. The majestic 12-branched chandelier is scaled for the size of the room (see *page 31* for guidelines).

● A pair of sconces brightens the hall *above* without impeding traffic flow. Although sconces are appropriate almost anywhere, they are particularly useful when floor space is at a premium. Because eye-level sconces are so visible, pay special attention to both their light quality and appearance.

● A lantern *left* suspended from the second floor ceiling provides lighting for this foyer and its gracefully curving staircase. Additional fixtures in the high ceiling create a brightly lit gallery and lead the eye upward. On any stairway, it is important that there be sufficient light for guests and family to negotiate the steps safely. Most codes require that three-way switches for stair lights be installed at both the top and bottom.

▌DESIGN TIP An entry hall is the ideal spot to spend a little extra on interesting fixtures simply because you don't need many. A huge variety of sconces and chandeliers is available at lighting and specialty stores. Or, check antiques shops or architectural salvage dealers for vintage fixtures (always rewire them before you install them).

living room

As gathering places for family and friends, living rooms need to accommodate groups both large and small with warmth, comfort, and style. Your lighting can help.

livingrooms

BALANCED LIGHTING. Friends and especially family tend to respond to the ambience of a living room—it can be a forbidding no-man's-land or a pleasant, inviting place to sit and share good conversation. The right lighting often makes all the difference.

● The living room on *pages 56–57* uses a variety of lighting sources for maximum flexibility and impact. All lamps and fixtures have dimmers to set any desired mood.

● Serene in its commitment to white and wide-open spaces, this living area owes much of its heavenliness to the indirect lighting that lines the room *right*. Broad expanses of French doors with transoms welcome the light that pours in during the day, and the pale walls and furnishings maximize its effect. But when daylight fades, valance cove lighting bounces off the ceiling and bathes the walls in a gentle glow. Strategically placed recessed lights with eyeball trims accent art on the walls, and a lamp behind the sofa furnishes additional light for conversation.

■DESIGN TIP Just because a room boasts a lot of natural light doesn't mean it needs minimal lighting. Plan to include general, task, and accent lighting in every room, so each area will be as livable after dark as it is in the daytime.

Awash with light from fixtures recessed in the ceiling, the walls *left* come alive with the dramatic interplay of light and dark. Canister fixtures, available in several depths, can be recessed into ceilings of various thicknesses. Because a portion of the ceiling is dropped and provides ample space, a standard size is used here. In rooms that have less than 8 inches of vertical space above the ceiling, use low-clearance fixtures. Some even fit in a space as shallow as 4 inches high.

A pair of contemporary sconces flank a tone-on-tone painting in the sophisticated sitting area *below.* The sconces were carefully positioned to shine at the midpoint of the canvas.

■DESIGN TIP As with any built-in lighting, it pays to prewire sconces during construction, even if you don't install them right away. Hide wiring behind the wall; add boxes and install the fixtures later.

DEFINED WITH LIGHT. More than any other single design element, light gives form and shape to spaces. Not only does the right lighting highlight architectural features, it defines and separates specific living areas. Fixtures mounted high on the walls or ceiling pull the eye upward to reveal the full extent of the room's space. A splash of light thrown upward accents a dramatic ceiling or the paneling of a tall wall. A large, high-ceilinged room needs the definition only light can provide.

In the barrel-vaulted room *opposite,* artificial and natural light sources combine to accentuate the shape and volume of the space. Set below the semicircular clerestory windows, two wall-mounted sconces shine upward to illuminate the curved ceiling. A row of recessed eyeball fixtures lights a pair of paintings for better viewing. Several downlights, used instead of a chandelier over the dining table, furnish abundant light.

MIX AND MATCH TRIMS. The basic canister-shaped recessed fixture, often called a "can light," is the same for both downlights and eyeball lights. The cylindrical can channels all the light downward, but you can dramatically alter the pattern the light throws in two ways: by choosing a different trim to aim, reflect, or diffuse the light, or by replacing the lightbulb inside with one of a different shape or color. Some trims have a glass diffuser that hides the bulb; others allow the bulb to remain visible.

● "Eyeball" fixtures aim the light directly at the painting over the fireplace *below left* and swivel to the exact position desired. A type called

a "wall washer" blocks a portion of the light to throw a shadow, a dramatic technique that is especially effective if you wish to accent the texture of a stone or brick wall.

● Recessed lights whose trim is flush with the ceiling *below right* provide more overall lighting than those with an eyeball or wall-washer trim. Most of these fixtures require lightbulbs of no more than 75 watts, but you can use a spotlight, a minispot, a regular incandescent, or a halogen bulb for different effects. Try a silver- or gold-color cone reflector trim for maximum light, or a black baffle trim for subdued mood lighting.

■ **DESIGN TIP** A basic recessed fixture with standard reflector trim throws light downward in a cone shape, producing a circle of light at the bottom as wide as the room is high. In a room with 8-foot ceilings, place the fixtures in a grid from 6 to 8 feet apart (and never closer than 4) so the light slightly overlaps. In a room with 10-foot ceilings, place them about 7 to 10 feet apart.

■ If you use a diffuser on a recessed light, you need a bulb with twice as much wattage to provide the same light as a bare bulb, but the light will appear softer.

A FORMAL AFFAIR. Traditional rooms can have lighting that ranges from authentic period antiques to the most contemporary fixtures. Often, in fact, the blend of styles is what gives the room an interesting twist.

● Perfectly in keeping with its sunny-yellow setting *opposite above,* the vintage gaslight fixture is original to the house but has since been wired for electricity. Italian metal lamps with translucent silk shades offer diffused light for reading or conversation. The candle sconce beside the window is for decoration only.

● In the symmetrically balanced room *opposite below,* matching table lamps with crisp white shades flank the sofa. To keep a sense of symmetry, be sure to use identical bulbs in each lamp because light color and brightness can vary.

● Bridging the gap between traditional and contemporary style in a townhouse *above,* two sleek torchère lamps wear unusual shades with gently draped fabric around the edges. Recessed lights provide ample overall lighting.

■**DESIGN TIP** A recessed light almost disappears if you paint its outside rim to match the ceiling.

LIGHT IN THE BALANCE. Balance plays an important part in the lighting of a room. The three types of lighting—general, task, and accent—must work in harmony, with one not dominating at the expense of the other two. The combined effect should provide the most evenly balanced light and maximum versatility for different purposes, such as light for conversation, reading, or accenting a collection of favorite objects.

● Multiple light sources come together to create an open airy feeling in the large, high-ceilinged living room *above*. Cove lighting tucked behind a wide crown molding makes the ceiling "float" and provides soft overall illumination. Although tubular fluorescent lights are sometimes used for cove lighting, strips of tiny incandescent bulbs provide a warmer light and can be dimmed more easily. Well-placed table lamps provide specific pools of more intense light. Many table lamps take three-way bulbs, which allow a low setting for accent lighting, medium for general illumination, or high for reading. Some lamps feature a touch-type switch that turns the light on and off, as well as dims it—a feature that often comes in handy.

● Sconces on either side of the bay window *above* balance the natural light as well as provide general illumination in the evening. For flexibility, switch sconces separately from other room lights and add a dimmer switch for a range of light level choices.

● Well-lit artwork pulls the eye toward the room's focal point, such as the carved stone and wood fireplace *left*. Picture lights are especially useful in situations like this one where the location of exposed beams precludes the use of recessed light fixtures.

■DESIGN TIP Consider adding an electrical receptacle in the top of the mantel if you plan to use a picture light or a pair of small lamps. A mantel receptacle, also handy for holiday lighting, eliminates the need for unsightly extension cords.

diningareas

In today's multipurpose dining areas, lighting needs to be suitable not only for dining but for many other family activities. The right fixture isn't always a chandelier.

diningareas

NOT YOUR MOTHER'S STYLE. There was a time when the phrase "dining-room fixture" almost always meant a multiarmed chandelier, usually made of cast metal or tubular brass, perhaps with prisms, hanging over the center of the table. That's definitely not the case anymore. While there are certainly rooms in which such a fixture is still most appropriate, some decorating styles call for lighting that is more spare, more contemporary, or more individual. Luckily, an abundance of choices exists for every taste.

In the relaxed French-country dining room on *pages 68–69,* a ceiling fixture styled after a kerosene lamp hovers over the table. In the otherwise dark corner, a traditional wall sconce and table lamp prove that adding interesting fixtures is one way to add character to a room.

As pared-down as the furniture beneath it, the halogen fixture *right* is suspended from the tall ceiling by two slender, almost invisible, cables. Halogen lights give off brighter, whiter beams of light than incandescent bulbs, which by comparison, produce an almost yellow light. To keep halogen lights from appearing overly harsh, connect a dimmer to the wall switch. Then you can adjust the light to suit both your task and your mood.

DINING WITH LIGHT. In the dining room, so often used for entertaining, hanging one fixture in the middle of the ceiling isn't quite enough to create a dramatically lit room. Try a variety of fixtures to achieve your functional and decorative goals. Balance light from a hanging fixture with recessed ceiling lights that illuminate artwork, brighten a buffet, or visually expand the room.

Wall-washer fixtures over the sideboard in the traditional dining room *above* illuminate the painting while also providing light for the buffet. The recessed lights can be turned up with a dimmer switch for serving, then turned down during the meal. Small, flame-shape bulbs and their reflections on the prisms in the chandelier produce an attractive glow over the dining table but don't cause a glare.

A broad expanse of mirrors reflects light and visually expands the dining room *above*. Set below a high, arched window and above a built-in buffet, the mirrors offer the open look of windows when viewed from inside, yet screen the dining room from the neighboring house. Golden-lined black shades on the brass-and-blown glass chandelier make the light appear warmer with a minimum of glare.

Subtle light sources combine in the formal dining area *left*. Matching sconces draw the eye to a portrait on the wall. Hidden in the crown molding, cove lighting defines and visually raises the room's ceiling. A traditional hall light, fitted with one candle, hangs over the pedestal table. Mirrors behind the shelves reflect the light and add a sense of depth to the room.

■ **DESIGN TIP** When a chandelier's lightbulbs are unshaded, it's important to use low-wattage bulbs to reduce glare directly over the table. If greater general lighting is desired, supplement the chandelier with light from candles, sconces, or other fixtures in the room.

BLENDING NATURALLY. For maximum enjoyment and impact day or night, consider how to combine natural and artificial light. In these examples, large windows unfettered by voluminous treatments let in plenty of light during the day. Artificial light is a supplement, brightening corners and easing shadows.

⬤ French doors, sidelights, and a transom welcome natural light into the combination dining room and library *opposite*. Eyeball fixtures in the sloping ceiling accent objects on the built-in bookshelves. The chandelier, wrapped with vines, takes on a fanciful look. (Avoid contact between natural elements and hot bulbs.) Clip shades onto the bulbs for a quick, easy accent.

⬤ Three single fixtures *above* come together to make a major statement about the value of art and individuality. Whereas each of the fixtures would have been too small alone, together they create a stunning effect, made more so by the hand-painted design on the ceiling.

⬤ Cove lighting emphasizes the shape and height of the raised ceiling *left*, while the circular table echoes its shape. A delicate leaf-motif chandelier suspended over the table has white shades that add to the light, airy feel of the room. Outside, a high stucco wall provides privacy for diners, eliminating the need for window treatments inside.

◼DESIGN TIP Multiple light sources are preferable to a single, too-bright source.

THE MAIN EVENT. No single fixture is more closely identified with its space than the main light fixture in the dining room. Hanging above the table, at center stage, the chandelier is a highly visible fixture that must not only provide light but set the tone for the entire room as well. The right fixture can enhance the house and furnishings, but the wrong one can fight them and be a visually jarring element. Fortunately, a seemingly endless variety of lovely fixtures can be purchased at home centers and lighting stores.

● Diffused light gently falls from the triple-tier fixture over the round table *above left*. A grand floor-to-ceiling framed mirror reflects not only the room but also the light, almost doubling its effectiveness. Hanging a mirror is a classic way to maximize available light, a technique especially useful in apartments or other situations where it's not possible to replace the existing fixture with a brighter one.

A faux-alabaster pendant patterned after an early-20th-century fixture feels right at home in the Mission-style dining room *above center*. Whereas the original lamps (now antiques) were carved from actual alabaster—a white or banded mineral closely resembling marble, but more translucent—today's replicas are made from glass or, in some cases, synthetic materials. The newer fixtures look like the real thing, but they are less likely to chip and are much less expensive.

Life moves in a circle, at least in the dining room *above right*, where the sleek spun-aluminum fixture echoes the shape of the table and medallion-back chairs. Bulbs hidden in the lower bowl shine upward to the larger reflector, then bounce down to light the table. The result is a soft light that complements candlelight. A mirror placed over a seldom-used closet door adds height and depth, so the room seems larger and brighter than it really is.

■DESIGN TIP Free yourself from any preconceived notion of what a dining room fixture *should* look like. In today's lenient decorating climate, mixing and matching styles is perfectly acceptable. Equally important as style are a fixture's shape in relation to the table, its scale compared to the dimensions of the room, and whether it provides an appropriate amount of light for the activities it illuminates.

SEEING THE LIGHT. Compare the light from two types of bulbs—you may be surprised at the difference. Most incandescent bulbs add a yellowish cast to everything they light, whereas halogen bulbs give more light per watt and shed a whiter, brighter light. This brighter light seems almost too bright for many situations, so be sure to connect any halogen lighting, whether it's a lamp or an overhead fixture, to a dimmer switch.

● Custom-made from an aluminum I-beam, the one-of-a-kind halogen fixture *above* adds an industrial quality to a minimalist dining room. Positioned on cables, three movable halogen lights are bright enough for doing homework or other projects that require close work, as well as for dining. Aluminum sconces flanking the doors emphasize the columned wall.

● A simple halogen fixture bounces diffused light off the breakfast room ceiling, which is painted to contrast with the crisp white moldings *opposite above*. Two matching lamps illuminate the built-in server at night; during the daytime, sunlight abounds.

Although it has no central lighting fixture, the dining room *above* offers plenty of sources for more than adequate light. Cove lighting reflects from the ceiling, and recessed fixtures, including halogen puck lights under the cabinet, put task lighting exactly where it's needed.

An example of elegant simplicity, three pendant lights hang in strict formation above the glass-top table *left*. During the day, the lights are unobtrusive, and often unnecessary, but at night the halogen bulbs provide easily adjustable light for dining or other activities. Recessed fixtures highlight the texture of the brick wall and illuminate the built-in buffet.

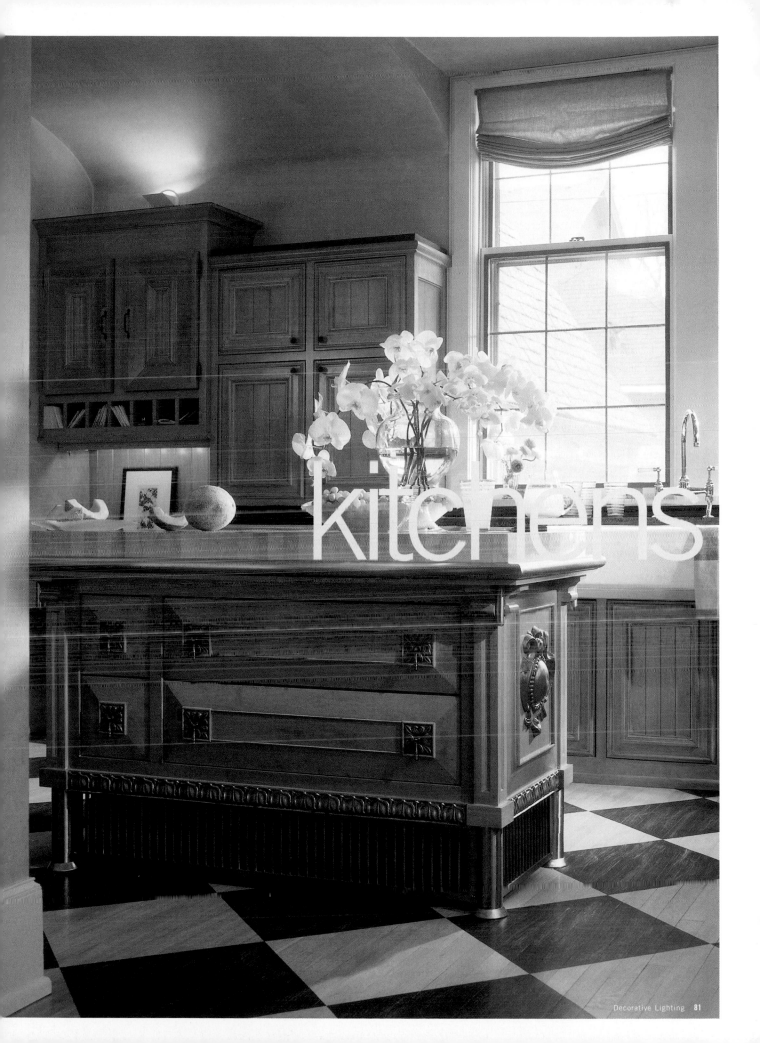

kitchens

Both a workplace and a room for casual entertaining, the kitchen must change its mood to suit the moment. A well-designed plan provides ideal lighting for every mood.

kitchens

OUT FOR RECESS. For overall lighting and for many task lighting situations in the kitchen, homeowners most often choose recessed downlights. Mounted flush with the ceiling, these fixtures don't break the surface plane of the ceiling as pendant lights or chandeliers do. Unlike surface-mounted fixtures, recessed ones don't make low ceilings seem lower. It's often best to team both recessed and hanging fixtures in rooms with higher ceilings for balanced lighting.

Architecturally interesting ceilings, such as the one in the kitchen on *pages 80–81,* deserve lighting that plays up their nonstandard features. Upward-shining sconces highlight the curved portions of the ceiling, while recessed lights provide general lighting over work spaces. Small fixtures built in under the cabinets are on separate switches to turn on only when needed.

A charming pendant is completely in character with the high-ceilinged kitchen *right* but doesn't provide nearly enough light for the room by itself. Supplemented by recessed fixtures in the ceiling and task lights under the cabinets and inside the range hood, it successfully sets the decorative tone for the kitchen.

DESIGN TIP When designing lighting for a building or remodeling project, imagine all the activities you'll do in the room and where you'll be doing them. Then plan accordingly, locating your fixtures exactly where you need them.

SOUL FOOD. Although a kitchen may be utilitarian, it's also the room where you spend a great deal of time, especially if you enjoy cooking. The most successful kitchens provide sustenance for the spirit as well as food for the body, and good lighting can play a part. Use light to showcase favorite possessions, such as china, glass, or artwork. Replace the center panels in upper cabinet doors with glass, then add lighting and glass shelves to draw attention to whatever is inside. Or place a few favorite objects on a slender shelf lit by lights beneath the cabinet. Rotate the pieces with others you enjoy for a room that's never boring.

DESIGN TIP When using glass shelves for display, place china plates and solid items against the back so they don't block light from reaching the shelves below. Display glass or smaller opaque items on any shelf, but put large vases on the lowest shelf for better balance.

● Cabinets become the focal point of the U-shape kitchen *opposite* through design, artisanship, and lighting. Built around an antique clock, the glass-front cabinets provide both storage and display space. Decorative trim above the doors is emphasized by the same lights that filter down through the glass shelves to the china and glass below. Undercabinet lights accent displayed items on a slim shelf. Ceiling-mounted downlights sparkle with faceted glass trim.

● Cove lighting installed above the cabinets creates a visual light show on the molding and ceiling *above*. Task lighting above the sink and cooktop also accents objects on the shelves. A fluorescent light and recessed lights over the island and pantry provide plenty of overall illumination.

■**DESIGN TIP** When planning cove lighting, consider the light pattern. You can use fluorescent lights (see *page 43*) or strings of tiny white lights in plastic tubes. Tube lights are easy to use in hard-to-reach areas, including the tops of cabinets—simply plug them in and lay them across the cabinet.

YOUR SPACE, YOUR STYLE. Most kitchens have lights in the ceiling, but the similarities end there. Some people prefer traditional options, some gravitate toward stripped-down types, and others go for the most creative fixtures they can find. Whatever your decorating style, you can choose primary fixtures that match your taste and fill in with less conspicuous fixtures for more balanced lighting.

Tiny halogen lights suspended from the ceiling provide task lighting with a lighthearted twist in the contemporary kitchen *below*. The round canopies mounted on the ceiling contain the transformers needed for each low-voltage lamp. Light flows through a raised glass breakfast bar, making it appear to float. Lights above the sloped top of the cabinet accent fluffy clouds painted on the ceiling.

Movable fixtures on a track provide general illumination in the kitchen *left* or can be aimed at more specific areas when needed. Recessed floodlights placed above work areas bypass the upper cabinets to light the countertop below. The stainless-steel hood not only vents steam, fumes, and cooking odors, it provides much-needed light above the range.

The alabaster-glass chandelier *below* works in tandem with recessed lights as it diffuses its soft glow over the table. Hang the fixture at a level that's comfortable and not imposing.

■DESIGN TIP When building an island, don't forget the electrical receptacles, handy for using appliances or for supplying power to small decorative lamps. A receptacle strategically placed in a cabinet ensures easy TV installation.

ALL IN THE FAMILY. You can buy track lights in a wide variety of shapes, styles, colors, and sizes. Several different types of fixtures can even be used on a single track for different purposes. In addition to standard incandescent fixtures, low-voltage halogen fixtures are available. But remember: Most fixtures work only on tracks made by the same manufacturer.

Exposed trusses support track lights in the open, airy kitchen *opposite above*. Each track is on the side, rather than the bottom, of the truss; the wiring is routed out of sight along the top of the of the truss. Note the use of different track fixtures.

A row of track lights offers flexible, easily adjustable lighting over the triangular island *opposite below*. Often a track can be wired to a ceiling box that previously had one fixture. That means several lights can go on the track without cutting more holes in the ceiling.

A continuous ceiling, broken only by a bay of cabinets suspended by rods, unifies the kitchen and family room *above*. Chrome-trimmed downlights used in the kitchen are repeated over the family-room entertainment center, allowing light to flow between the two spaces. Large line-voltage fixtures and smaller low-voltage halogen fixtures share the same ceiling-mounted track.

■DESIGN TIP When installing a ceiling fan *opposite above*, make sure existing lights don't shine through the revolving blades. This can cause a disturbing strobe-light effect.

PERHAPS A PENDANT. From incandescent bulbs with vintage-schoolhouse glass shades to ultrafuturistic halogen cones that pack a lot of brightness into tiny fixtures, hanging pendants remain some of the most popular choices for kitchen ceiling fixtures. Rarely used alone, they're often supplemented by other lighting that fills in where they leave off. Introduce pendants over an island or a countertop where low-hanging fixtures don't interfere with traffic flow.

● Raise or lower halogen lights over the kitchen island as needed *opposite*—notice the counterweights that keep the fixtures in place. Tracks around the perimeter of the ceiling support additional halogen lights, aimed strategically. Under-cabinet lights accent accessories and furnish extra task lighting.

● The vaulted wooden ceiling *right* doesn't seem at all oppressive because it is balanced by bright white walls and cabinets. Large windows and a skylight flood the room with natural light. A combination of translucent-glass pendant fixtures

and recessed lighting on each side of the room provides both ambient and task lighting. Angled ceilings necessitate using special trims on recessed fixtures so the light falls in the right direction; consult a lighting adviser about the best lighting for your particular ceiling.

● Two matching pendants hang directly over the kitchen island *left,* creating a bright place to eat or work. The main task lighting comes from downlights installed in the dropped, wooden portion of the ceiling. The higher central portion of the ceiling glows, thanks to hidden cove lights.

■**DESIGN TIP** Avoid locating kitchen lighting where you will have to work in your own shadow, or you'll have to fill in with light coming from sources in other directions.
■ Getting the light source closer to the work surface considerably increases the light intensity. A light hung 3 feet above a counter, for example, provides four times as much light on the surface as the same size light hung 6 feet away.

bed&bath

Not just for sleeping and bathing, these more private spaces need flexible lighting that can change from functional to romantic to suit the need and mood of the moment.

bed&bath

HIGHLIGHT YOUR STYLE. Choose lighting that works, both technically and aesthetically, with the decorative style of your bedrooms and baths. In sleek, contemporary rooms, use lighting to create an interplay of light and shadow for drama, but softer, more traditional rooms need gentle lighting to preserve their mood.

Glass-shelved cabinets come alive with halogen lights in the compact master bath on *pages 92–93.* The clear shelves let light from low-voltage fixtures shine all the way through to the bottom. Above the basin, two more tiny downlights supplement the task lighting from sconces that flank the mirror. For general illumination, a frosted-glass fixture hangs from the ceiling.

There's something calming about a clutter-free bedroom, and the right lighting scheme enhances the mood. Two ceiling-mounted fixtures act as lamps in the bedroom *right,* leaving space on the bedside tables for soul-soothing necessities such as flowers. A table lamp provides light for writing or other work at the desk.

■**DESIGN TIP** Lighting for built-in cabinets, such as those on *pages 92–93,* is best planned during construction, when all sides of the cabinets are accessible. The low-voltage fixtures used are quite small so they can be positioned exactly where desired. Some halogen fixtures measure only ¾ inch thick and fit flush into a hole drilled in the cabinet.

A RESTFUL PLACE TO UNWIND. Many people read for a while or relax in bed before falling asleep. Place all bedside lamps at a comfortable height and within arm's reach. Even built-in lighting should have controls that are easily accessible so you don't have to get out of bed to turn off the light.

Each of the table lamps *below* has two bulbs with separate pull switches, allowing users to adjust the light level up or down. For more flexibility, choose bulbs of different wattages, perhaps 60 and 25. Turn on both bulbs for reading, only the brighter bulb for an intermediate level, or only the dimmer bulb for mood lighting.

Recessed downlights mounted on the ceiling, about a foot out from the wall, supplement a pair of table lamps for bedside reading *left*. A sconce on a dimmer provides mood lighting, and blinds provide both light control and privacy.

Many bedrooms don't have any ceiling fixtures and must rely on lamps alone. One outlet is usually connected to the switch so someone entering the room can immediately turn on a light. If this is the case in your room, position enough lamps to light the room evenly.

■DESIGN TIP Bedside lamps needn't match exactly but should complement each other. Choose fixtures of roughly the same height or purchase matching shades to unify them.

AT THE MIRROR. For shaving and applying makeup, concentrate on lighting the face, not the mirror. Plan carefully: Will you be standing or sitting? How tall are you? How close will you be to the mirror? Usually the best solution is a mixture of task lighting and general illumination that increases the overall light level, with each fixture on separate controls. Use dimmers so you can adjust the light level as needed.

Two surface-mounted fixtures above the twin basins emit soft, yet directional, lighting *below*. The fixtures are mounted close to the mirror to highlight the face of a person standing in front of the counter. Centering the fixtures above the sinks gives even lighting from both sides. A fixture of similar shape (but rated for a damp location as required by most electrical codes) lights the shower stall.

Mounting light fixtures on a mirror, as in the bath *above,* requires coordination between the electrician and mirror supplier. First locate, install, and wire the electrical boxes, then measure for the mirror and drill holes in the glass to match the boxes. With the mirror in place, install the fixtures.

Expansive facing mirrors make the most of whatever light you have, reflecting it back and forth infinitely. A sconce on each side of the dressing table *left* proves the point. Recessed lighting and a skylight in the center of the room offer well-balanced lighting throughout.

■DESIGN TIP The color of surfaces and appliances greatly affects a room's lighting. Light that bounces off a red wall, for example, has a red cast. When the color of light is critical, as it is in a dressing area, stick with a neutral color scheme for walls, ceiling, and flooring.

ONCE UPON A TIME. In recent years, pedestal sinks and vintage-look porcelain sinks have returned to popularity, but does this mean you must choose old-fashioned lighting fixtures? Not at all! Any style will do as long as it throws an even light on the area. Petite sconces placed at about eye level are more than adequate in the room *left* because other light sources provide general illumination. The fixtures are capped with matching clip-on shades that soften the glare.

Tautly stretched cables suspend three halogen lights above the basin *left*. The lights, although tiny, are movable and can be aimed to throw light exactly where it's needed.

Up or down, it really doesn't matter which way many glass-shaded fixtures are mounted. When installed shade-down, as shown *above,* light comes through the translucent (or transparent) shade and the bulb is visible from below. When installed shade-up, the light still shines through the glass, and it bounces off the ceiling.

■DESIGN TIP Update an old bathroom fixture or give a new one more character by changing its shade. Home improvement stores offer numerous styles, from etched-glass traditional to sculptured contemporary. Make sure the base of the one you choose is the right size for your fixture. It's a good idea to buy an extra shade, in case one breaks. Antiques shops sell shades with unusual shapes and coloring, but be prepared to pay more.

FOR YOUR GUESTS. Lighting requirements are the same for a guest bath as for the master bath—just remember to locate the switches and dimmer controls in easy-to-find places.

● A single three-light fixture is easy to install above a mirror *top left*. Strip fixtures come in many lengths and styles.

● A pair of sconces flanks the decorative mirror *top right*. Always mount this type of sconce, and others that shine upward, above eye level so the bulb doesn't show.

● Outdoor lanterns bring a gardenlike feeling to the powder room *bottom right*. If using clear glass fixtures, select frosted bulbs to reduce the glare. To reduce it further, use bulbs with less wattage or install a dimmer.

● The walls and ceiling of the bath *opposite* are decidedly "in the pink," but plentiful natural light, a broad expanse of mirror, sconces with neutral shades, and lots of white woodwork keep the room from experiencing a rosy overdose.

■**DESIGN TIP** When building or remodeling, run wiring for sconces during the rough-in stage, then cover it with drywall. Later, after you hang a framed mirror, you can determine the exact location of the fixtures. Then cut holes for the boxes, pull out the wiring, and install the boxes and fixtures. This method allows the greatest flexibility in placing fixtures.

special places

Some rooms don't fit the neat categories of living room, dining room, and kitchen. Because these special spaces often serve multiple functions, they need flexible lighting that accommodates a variety of uses.

special places

QUALITY THROUGHOUT. Many people put a lot of thought into choosing fixtures for the main rooms in their homes, but when it comes to other areas—home offices, basement or attic remodelings, and all the niches found in a typical dwelling—they aren't as discerning. The lighting in these minor areas is equally as important to make your home as functional as possible.

A true art lover always rejoices when favorite pieces are displayed to advantage with the appropriate lighting. Because very few people live in museums, balancing the lighting necessary for art with the needs of a normal household can present a challenge. Halogen lights on standard ceiling tracks work well in both rooms on *pages 104–105*, angling gallery-type lighting toward paintings, yet providing general room lighting as well.

Used mainly for watching television and curling up by the fire, the family room *right* has lighting that adjusts up or down with dimmers. Several types of recessed lights surround the room: Wall washers maximize the texture of fieldstone walls, small spotlights highlight accessories, and ceiling floodlights provide general lighting. Cove lighting adds drama at night.

DESIGN TIP Lighting is an investment that lasts for decades, so don't skimp on wiring for fixtures when building or remodeling. Go ahead and prewire when it's inexpensive to do so, then connect decorative fixtures as your budget allows.

A HAPPY HOME. The pleasures of living in a well-lit home don't lessen, even with time. Beautiful, functional lighting makes a difference every single day in the way you live and how you feel about your home.

● The bar *above,* designed for entertaining, features a curved ceiling echoed by an arched cabinet. Recessed downlights, including one centered over the sink, provide task lighting and accent the glassware on the shelves. Puck-style halogen lights brighten the inside of the glass-front cabinets. A track fixture in the adjoining sewing room pivots to light the work surface.

● Books share wall space with generous windows in the spacious library *above center.* A pair of brass swing-arm floor lights stands ready beside reading chairs that flank the fireplace. Rows of tiny lights hidden behind the crown molding heighten the already raised ceiling and create an especially dramatic effect at night.

● Undercabinet halogen lights mounted beneath built-in bookshelves illuminate the sofa for reading while accenting the three framed paintings below them *above right.* Swing-arm lamps mounted on the sidewalls leave the tabletops free for other objects.

● With a small, bumped-out addition, the bedroom *opposite* gains a comfortable nook for lounging or nature-watching, multidirectional windows, and extensive storage. Spotlights aim the light for reading.

■**DESIGN TIP** In a library, you need light to read and also to illuminate the titles on the shelves. This usually requires a mix of general lighting and lamps.

COZY CORNERS. All you need to create a restful refuge is comfortable seating, a good book, and the right lighting. You don't need a lot of space—smaller is often better. *Clockwise from upper left:*

● A candlelit lantern, for mood, and a lantern-lamp hanging from a hook illuminate a Swedish daybed tucked under the eaves.

● A lowered ceiling has recessed downlights that provide light for reading; the floodlight bulbs create scallops of light over the art.

● Built-in seating turns a stair landing into a nook for reading the books on nearby shelves. A pair of swing-arm lamps high on the wall lights both the seating area and the bookshelves.

● Floor-to-ceiling bookshelves transform formerly wasted space at the end of a landing. Recessed downlights a foot from the face of the shelves accent books and art. A ceiling fixture lights the hallway.

● Oversize picture lights above bookshelves provide light for browsing as well as illumination for dining. The table can be positioned for studying or for parties.

● Recessed lights with metal covers team with uplights shining on the sloped ceiling to create a dramatic effect in a study.

● Low-wattage pendant lamps and recessed can lights make a home office a delight to work in—even when natural light isn't flooding through the windows and door.

CONTRIBUTORS

Contributing Photographers: Cheryl Dalton, Tria Giovan, Bob Greenspan, Emily Minton
Contributing Project Designers: Brian Carter (*pages 18–20, 32 left, 33*), Wade Scherrer (*pages 21, 44 top left, 45 top left*)

U.S. UNITS TO METRIC EQUIVALENTS

To Convert From	Multiply By	To Get
Inches	25.4	Millimeters (mm)
Inches	2.54	Centimeters (cm)
Feet	30.48	Centimeters (cm)
Feet	0.3048	Meters (m)

METRIC UNITS TO U.S. EQUIVALENTS

To Convert From	Multiply By	To Get
Millimeters	0.0394	Inches
Centimeters	0.3937	Inches
Centimeters	0.0328	Feet
Meters	3.2808	Feet